From _____

Other books by Exley:

Daughters ...   For a Good Friend
Missing You ...   To my Husband
Sisters ...   When Love is Forever
True Love ...

Dedicated to Momtom

Published simultaneously in 1996 by Exley Publications in Great Britain, and Exley Giftbooks in the USA.

12   11   10   9

Border illustrations by Juliette Clarke
Copyright © Helen Exley 1996
The moral right of the author has been asserted.

ISBN 1-85015-695-6

Edited and pictures selected by Helen Exley.

Picture research by Image Select International.
Typeset by Delta, Watford.
Printed in China.

Exley Publications Ltd, 16 Chalk Hill, Watford, Herts. WD1 4BN.
Exley Publications LLC, 232 Madison Avenue, Suite 1206, NY 10016, USA.

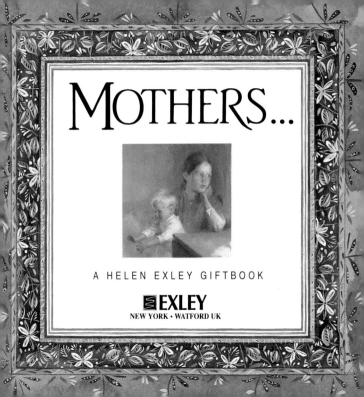

MOTHERS...

A HELEN EXLEY GIFTBOOK

EXLEY
NEW YORK · WATFORD UK

WHAT MAKES A MOTHER?

A mother can be almost any size or any age, but she won't admit to anything over thirty. A mother has soft hands and smells good. A mother likes new dresses, music, a clean house, her children's kisses, an automatic washer and Daddy. A mother doesn't like having her children sick, muddy feet, temper tantrums, loud noise or bad report cards.

*A mother can read a thermometer (much to the
amazement of Daddy) and like magic, can
kiss a hurt away.*

*A mother can bake good cakes and pies but likes
to see her children eat vegetables.*

*A mother can stuff a fat baby into a snow suit in
seconds and can kiss sad little faces and
make them smile.*

AUTHOR UNKNOWN

The heart of a mother is a deep abyss at the
bottom of which you will always discover
forgiveness.

HONORÉ DE BALZAC

There shall never be another quite so
tender, quite so kind as the patient little
mother, nowhere on this earth you'll find
her affection duplicated....

PAUL C. BROWNLOW

In a child's lunch box, a mother's thoughts.

JAPANESE PROVERB

A MOTHER …

… is the lady who looks surprised and delighted
when her children bring her breakfast at
four o'clock on Mother's Day.

… has ten pairs of arms. She has to.

… is the elegant woman with chewed rusk in the
embroidery of her evening gown.

… is the person you need when absolutely
no one else will do.

… is the woman on the beach putting the final
touch to a sand version of Mad King Ludwig of
Bavaria's most extravagant castle – while her children
sit throwing stones at sticks.

… stands No Nonsense. Well not *much*.

… is the lady who can talk comforting nonsense that somehow makes things better.

… is the lady with drawers jammed with finger paintings, letters, handmade greetings cards, lopsided Easter bunnies, clay cats, certificates and medals. And who could not be persuaded to part with one of them.

… is someone who has learned to love and can never after get out of the habit.

… is the one who goes white when the phone rings at 11 at night.

… is a lady who can do a dozen things at once – and still find time to kiss a bruised knee better.

PAM BROWN, b.1928

"You are the caretaker of the generations, you are the birth giver," the sun told the woman. "You will be the carrier of this universe."

BRULE SIOUX, SUN CREATION MYTH

When God thought of Mother, he must have laughed with satisfaction, and framed it quickly so rich, so deep, so divine, so full of soul, power and beauty, was the conception.

HENRY WARD BEECHER

Most of all the other beautiful things

in life come by twos and threes, by dozens

and hundreds. Plenty of roses, stars,

sunsets, rainbows, brothers and sisters,

aunts and cousins, but only one mother in

the whole world.

KATE DOUGLAS WIGGIN

$\mathcal{A}$ mother's love for the child of her body differs essentially from all other affections, and burns with so steady and clear a flame that it appears like the one unchangeable thing in this earthly mutable life, so that when she is no longer present it is still a light to our steps and a consolation.

W. H. HUDSON (1841-1922)

A mother's love! What can compare with it!
Of all things on earth, it comes nearest to
divine love in heaven.
A mother's love means a life's devotion –
and sometimes a life's sacrifice – with but
one thought, one hope and one feeling,
that her children will grow up healthy and
strong, free from evil habits and able to
provide for themselves.

ANONYMOUS

To my mother I tell the truth. I have no thought, no feeling that I cannot share with my mother, and she is like a second conscience to me, her eyes like a mirror reflecting my own image.

WILLIAM GERHARDIE (1895-1977)

... she fed our oafish wits with steady, imperceptible shocks of beauty. Though she tortured our patience and exhausted our nerves, she was, all the time, building up around us, by the unconscious revelations of her loves, an interpretation of man and the natural world so unpretentious and easy that we never recognized it then, yet so true that we never forgot it.

his these
2 pages

Bear Print ®
JACKSON HOLE, WYOMING
307-733-1558

Nothing now that I ever see that has the edge of gold around it – the change of a season, a jewelled bird in a bush, the eyes of orchids, water in the evening, a thistle, a picture, a poem – but my pleasure pays some brief duty to her. She tried me at times to the top of my bent. But I absorbed from birth, as now I know, the whole earth through her jaunty spirit.

LAURIE LEE, b.1914,
FROM *"CIDER WITH ROSIE"*

Where there is a mother in the house,
matters speed well.

AMOS BRONSON ALCOTT

The most vivid memories of my youth
are linked with my mother's kitchen
coming home to warmth of a log fire and
good food, lovingly prepared.

MARGARET FULTON

Mothers are the people who can work
flat out all day – and be back where
they were the night before.

MARION GARRETTY, b.1917

One of my children wrote in a third-grade
piece on how her mother spent her time …
"one-half time on home, one-half time on
outside things, one-half time writing."

CHARLOTTE MONTGOMERY

Now, as always, the most automated
appliance in a household is the mother.

BEVERLEY JONES, b.1927

Any mother could perform the jobs of
several air traffic controllers with ease.

LIS ALTHER, b.1944

One moment makes a father, but a mother is made
by endless moments, load on load.

JOHN G. NEIHARDT

Round the idea of one's mother, the mind of man clings with fond affection. It is the first thought stamped upon our infant hearts, when yet soft and capable to receiving the most profound impressions, and all the after feelings of the world are more or less light in comparison. I do not know that even in our old age we do not look back to that feeling as the sweetest we have ever known through life.

CHARLES DICKENS (1812-1870),
FROM *"ALL YEAR ROUND"*

My first vivid memory ... is ... when first I looked into her face and she looked into mine. That I do remember, and that exchanging look I have carried with me all my life. We recognized each other. I was her child and she was my mother.... What I inherited from my mother is inside me. I love people too easily, as she did. For this gift of loving, I thank my beloved mother.

PEARL S. BUCK (1892-1973)

WORRY, WORRY

$\mathcal{M}$others are strange creatures. It's true.

Even when their kids are going grey or bald or both they worry about their underwear. And socks. And summer colds.

They worry when the roads are icy. Or when there's an epidemic. They worry about childish weaknesses long outgrown. They are stunned to find their children so precocious. They feel the same astonishment when their sons are appointed Chairman

of the Board as when they won the sack race.

They are flabbergasted and delighted when their

little daughters become headteachers.

They need to keep in touch.

They phone at inconvenient moments.

They smile bright crocodile smiles at friends of whom

they don't approve.

They refuse to grow old peacefully.

PAM BROWN, b.1928

Dear Mother: I'm all right.
Stop worrying about me.

EGYPTIAN PAPYRUS LETTER, c.2000 B.C.

Human mothers are the only ones to allow
their offspring to go on worrying them for
their entire lives.

PAM BROWN, b.1928

Because I am a mother, I am capable of
being shocked; as I never was when I was
not one.

MARGARET ATWOOD, b.1939

Love … had a strange way of multiplying.
Doubling. Trebling itself, so that, as each
child arrived, there was always more than
enough to go around.

ROSAMUNDE PILCHER, b.1924

The only explanation for the unselfishness,
sacrifice, loyalty and tenderness of
motherhood is love.

LEROY BROWNLOW,
FROM *"FLOWERS FOR MOTHER"*

Mothers ask little of you:
Say please and thank you.
Always carry a clean handkerchief.
Wear mended underwear.
Wash the back of your neck.
Don't show off. Arrive on time.
Don't outstay your welcome.
Eat nicely.
Never waste food.
Be kind to animals.
It is imprinted indelibly on the mind and
heart and soul.
Forever.

PAM BROWN, b.1928

*N*ever lend your car to anyone to whom
you have given birth.

ERMA BOMBECK, b.1927

The first time your baby says "Ma-Maaaa,"
your heart leaps.
Fifteen years later you wish she'd turn it
down a little.

MARION GARRETTY, b.1917

Ask your child what he wants for dinner only if
he's buying.

FRAN LEBOWITZ

A suburban mother's role is to deliver children
obstetrically once, and by car for ever after.

PETER DE VRIES, b.1910

There never was a child so lovely but his mother
was glad to get him asleep.

RALPH WALDO EMERSON (1803-1882)

TO MY MOTHER

You are like an everlasting friendship.
You are like a secret almost
too wonderful to keep.
You are like the beginning, end, and everything
in between.
You are like a spring shower.
You are like the sun shining on me and
keeping me warm.
You are like a wild flower in a meadow.
You are like a very knowledgeable volume
of encyclopedias.
You are like you and I love you.

LAUREL O. HOYE, AGE 8

SHE SEES THROUGH YOU

She does have a knack for penetrating disguises,

whether it be small boys who claim that they have

taken baths or middle-aged daughters who swear

that they have lost five pounds.

Some time ago I had a collection of short pieces

brought out in book form and I sent one of the

first copies to Mother. She was naturally

delighted. Her enthusiasm fairly bubbled off the

pages of the letter. "Darling," she wrote, "isn't it

marvelous the way those old pieces of yours finally

came to the surface like a dead body!"

JEAN KERR, b.1923, FROM *"MY WILD IRISH MOTHER"*

They always looked back before turning the corner, for their mother was always at the window to nod and smile, and wave her hand at them. Somehow it seemed as if they couldn't have got through the day without that, for whatever their mood might be, the last glimpse of that motherly face was sure to affect them like sunshine.

LOUISA MAY ALCOTT (1832-1888),
FROM *"LITTLE WOMEN"*

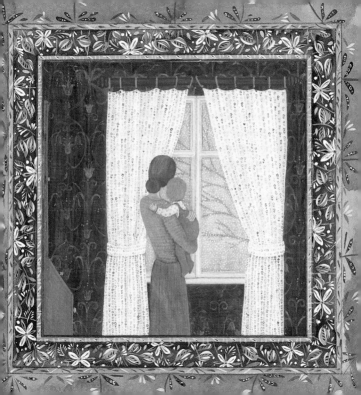

Housework, sewing, customers: how, when
you have your work always in your hands, do
you keep four children from straying?… She
kept us on the long leash of an endless rope
of language, looping and knotting us as
firmly to her as ever she stitched edge to edge
in a seam.… Like a conjurer she kept us
busy, kept us interested, kept us occupied,
kept us fascinated, winding us in endless
strings of reciprocal talk, ropes of argument,
singing necklaces, bracelets of laughter,

looping us with garments of language,

bejewelling us with glittering sentences,

bubbling and streaming ideas and thoughts

and discussion and exhortations and

moralizings, and sometimes, when we'd

briefly slipped the spell, an anxious crying of

our names up and down the block, or a stern

motherly shout or two.

ADELE WISEMAN, b.1928,
FROM *"OLD WOMAN AT PLAY"*

One part of a mother's mind is constantly upon her children however adult, however sophisticated they may have become. She studies, calculates, arranges, runs enterprises, writes books, deals with patients, gives sound professional advice.

But, always, a little section of her brain is reserved for family matters and at every pause in the pressures of the day will turn to such concerns as slipped discs, mortgages, pregnancies, and the recipe for carrot cake she promised.

PAM BROWN, b.1928

I owe this woman the supreme debt. Life itself. I have no doubt, given the deplorable circumstances surrounding my first three years, that had a lesser person held my life in her hands … I would not have survived. Not only did she give me life … she taught me how to *live* life. Right from wrong; fairness and consideration for others. The kind of values that make the world a better place. It is not enough to say Ian Leslie was lucky to have such a Mum. He was blessed.

IAN LESLIE, FROM *"MUM'S THE WORD"*

A woman's love is mighty,
but a mother's heart is weak.
And by its weakness overcomes.

JAMES RUSSELL LOWELL

Mums are an interlocking chain
that holds the world together.

PAM BROWN, b.1928

Whoever heard of Father Earth?

VANCE BOURJAILY

… although she's self-effacing and
sometimes in fragile health, whenever
I'm with her I feel as secure as a cub
protected by its lioness.

GEOFFREY ROBERTSON,
FROM *"MUM'S THE WORD"*

The mildest, gentlest, kindliest mother,
when confronted by someone who could
harm her children, snarls, attacks, bites,
claws – and spits them out.

PAM BROWN, b.1928

… even as a child you knew you were being led,

and as you grew older you sometimes suspected

you were being taken, but who could resist?

Who wanted to miss anything? You knew she

was building a glittering web to contain you but

you knew you were always at its centre … and

she might be controlling you but she was also

completely at your service, helping you learn to

work the controls that would take you farther.…

ADELE WISEMAN, b.1928,
FROM "OLD WOMAN AT PLAY"

There's no such thing as the archetypal mother save in the purely biological sense. There are as many sorts of mother as there are women. Gentle, ferocious, brainy, dim, somnolent, hyperactive, smiling, grim. Disciplinarians or prone to laissez-faire. Ambitious and driving or accepting the fact that their happy, smiling piglets will never learn to fly.

Some destroy. But most, in one fashion or another, raise their children and send them on their way with the best gift that anyone can give. The certainty of love.

CHARLOTTE GRAY, b.1937

It was from you that I first learned to
think, to feel, to imagine, to believe….

JOHN STERLING (1806-1844),
IN A LETTER TO HIS MOTHER

My mother succeeded in making me
understand a great deal … indeed I owe to
her loving wisdom, all that was bright and
good in my long night.

HELEN KELLER (1880-1968),
FROM "THE STORY OF MY LIFE"

*O*ver the years, whenever praise came my way, she was always thunderingly silent, even though I suspected she was pleased. When I eventually asked her about this, she said she should be an equaliser to avoid me becoming big-headed!

There's nothing of the cliché "stage mother" about mine!

Now, aged eighty-four, she doesn't have to say anything; whenever she's pleased her beautiful face beams her approval and pleasure – no words are necessary.

DENNIS OLSEN, FROM *"MUM'S THE WORD"*

Acknowledgements: The publishers are grateful for permission to reproduce copyright material. Whilst every effort has been made to trace copyright holders, the publishers would be pleased to hear from any not here acknowledged. PEARL S. BUCK: extract from "Pearl S. Buck" by Theodore F. Harris published by Methuen, a division of Reed International; JEAN KERR: extract from "My Wild Irish Mother" taken from "The Snake Has All The Lines" © 1960 The McCall Corporation. Reprinted by permission of Doubleday, a division of Bantam Doubleday Dell Publishing Group; LAURIE LEE: extract from "Cider With Rosie" published by Penguin Books 1962 © Laurie Lee 1959. Reprinted with permission of Peters, Fraser and Dunlop Group Ltd.; IAN LESLIE: extract from "Mum's The Word" published by North Rocks Press, 1986; DENNIS OLSEN: extract from "Mum's The Word" published by North Rocks Press, 1986; NELLY SACHS: extract from "The Seeker And Other Poems" published by Farrar, Straus and Giroux and Suhrkamp Verlag; ADELE WISEMAN: extracts from "Old Woman At Play" taken from "Mother To Daughter, Daughter To Mother" by Tilly Olsen published by Virago Press Ltd. Reprinted by permission of the author.

Picture Credits: Exley Publications is very grateful to the following individuals and organizations for permission to reproduce their pictures: Archiv für Kunst (AKG), Bridgeman Art Library (BAL),